CRUISE
SHIPS
DO
FUNNY
THINGS
TO
ME

JOSHUA KINSER

This one's for me. You're always there for me when I need you. Even when you don't feel like it.

A portion of the author's proceeds will be donated to Mercy Ships, a global charity that has operated hospital ships in developing nations since 1978.

Mercy Ships brings hope and healing to the forgotten poor by mobilizing people and resources worldwide, and serving all people without regard for race, gender, or religion. Mercy Ships programs promote health and well-being by serving the urgent surgical needs of the forgotten poor and empowering developing communities. Since its founding, Mercy Ships has performed more than 1.7 million services valued at over $670 million and impacting more than 1.9 million people as direct beneficiaries.

For more information on Mercy Ships, visit their website at: www.mercyships.org.

"Never be afraid to try something new. Remember that a lone amateur built the Ark. A large group of professionals built the *Titanic*."

—Dave Barry

CRUISE
SHIPS
DO
FUNNY
THINGS
TO
ME

ONE

EVERYTHING IS MUCH BETTER IN THE BAHAMAS

I always bring a pack of pens along with me on the plane whenever I travel to the Bahamas. All different colored pens: sea-foam green, coconut brown, sunshine yellow, Customs-and-Immigration-holding-cell blue—all the colors of the Bahamian rainbow. You see, once upon a time, in a Latin country called Miami, I boarded a plane on a hot summer day, and I took wing over the Caribbean Sea. It was a little puddle jumper of a plane, the kind you see pictured in newspaper articles with headlines like, *Midday Plane Crash, No Survivors.*

As the plane drifted toward the patchy cotton-ball clouds, I watched all the little islands off the coast of Florida—each of them with beach cottages painted the same neon colors that you find on poisonous snakes and spiders in the Amazon—shrink into small dots among a vast expanse of deep blue sea.

I was being transferred. Catching my next cruise ship in Nassau. And I was on a tight schedule. The ship was scheduled to set sail at around four p.m. My forty-five minute flight from Miami to the Bahamas left at one p.m. That gave me three hours to get through customs and get aboard that cruise liner. I was on ship time, and I knew that the captain waits for no man.

After a few minutes in the air, I drifted asleep. I didn't wake up until I heard the sound of plane tires screeching to a halt. Outside my window, the coconut palms that bordered the tarmac were blowing in the breeze. *Caribbean life, baby.* I'm always willing to travel for decent work. Especially when the job is on board a cruise ship with the bow pointed toward the tropics.

Off my flight tray, I grabbed the little square sheet of paper with a heading at the top that read *IMMIGRATION FORM.* One of the friendly Bahamian airline stewards must have left it there for me, not wanting to wake me up as they passed them out. *How nice.*

I stepped off the plane and grabbed my bags from among the luggage out on the runway. I pulled down my shades and walked into the airport terminal.

Big banner sign: *WELCOME TO THE BAHAMAS.* I felt a blast of air conditioning. A steel drum ensemble with a female singer played Lionel Ritchie's "All Night Long" as I walked in.

Yes. Wonderful. What a welcome! All I needed was a guy with dreadlocks selling fresh steamed lobsters and little cups of butter, and I would have been in heaven. I could smell the beach from there.

I had been the last one off the plane, and so when I walked into the terminal, I was at the end of the line of people waiting to get through Customs. I watched as every one ahead of me breezed through without a problem. Customs: just a slight inconvenience, and a small price to pay for an all-access pass to paradise.

There was a long line of customs workstations, like an electric fence to keep the gringo goats from freely grazing on the green Bahamian grass on the other side, but there was only one woman working behind a single station.

The moment I stepped up to the counter, the steel drum band stopped playing, as if they had been contracted to play only until the last person walked up to the counter. Just like a band, never playing a second more than they're paid for. That last tinny note of the steel drum echoed through the terminal. The band walked out the back door, and the room became deathly quiet. It felt larger than it had before, now that it was just me and the customs agent, all alone on the edge of Nassau.

I put my Customs and Immigration form on the counter and noticed that the agent had a pen clipped onto the front pocket of her shirt. I looked at her and smiled. "Do you have a pen I could use to fill out the immigration form?"

She did not smile back. Red flag number one.

She pointed to my form on the counter. "What is dis (this)?"

What an odd question. Has she not seen a customs form before? "Um, this is my immigration form."

"Why it not be filled out?"

"Um, well see, I didn't have a pen, and I must have fallen asleep. I—"

She pointed to the form, to a section near the top. I looked down and read it. It said something like: *All persons entering the Bahamas must fill out and sign Immigration and Customs form and have form in hand at all times prior to entering the country.*

"I'm really sorry," I said. "I seem to have fallen asleep. If I could just use your pen I—"

"I don't have no pen."

"Actually, there is a pen right there on your shirt. If I could just use it, I'll—"

She looked down at her shirt pocket. "Dis is my pen. Why don't you have no pen to fill out de form?"

Was I still dreaming? Should I try and slap myself awake? What kind of bizarre-o world had I awoken to here? I felt as if I was in a *Seinfeld* episode. *No pen for you.*

I looked around at the other security stations. No pens. No pencils. No crayons, even. "Are there any other pens in here that I could use?"

"I *don't* know. Keeping track of pens for you isn't my job."

Geesh. Wouldn't you know it? I'm on a tight schedule to catch a ship that's pulling out of harbor in T-minus two hours, and I'm trapped inside the Bahamian air terminal with the pen Nazi.

I grabbed my form, admittedly displaying a bit of frustration and disbelief, which certainly didn't help my cause. I walked toward the back of the terminal, toward a waist-high bench running the length of the back wall, the type of bench you see in banks that people use to fill out deposit slips. As I got closer, I saw one of those silver chains, the kind with the little beads, that you always see connected to (Could it be? Had I been saved?) pens.

I grabbed the chain. Nothing. I looked down the long counter. There was a line of chains, all of them just dangling off the end of the bench with no pens attached.

This place had been the victim of a crack pen burglar. I walked down the line, grabbing each chain as I went, hoping to find a pen on the end of one of the chains. Nothing. Just lousy silver beads that I could spin in my hand. I rummaged through my bags. Nothing.

I turned around to face her. She was waiting, like a shark circling my life raft, knowing that eventually I would fall overboard and eventually the shark would have its bloody meal. As long as she was patient, she knew she would win, because this shark had the only stupid pen in the sea.

I approached cautiously; this was going to require the diplomatic skills of a Naval war college graduate. She was writing something in a notepad—with her pen.

"I can't seem to find a pen anywhere," I said. "What would you suggest I do?"

"You cannot go through customs until de form is completed."

"So you want me to wait here until I can find a pen?"

"I don't care what you do, but you be not coming tru (through) here until dis form be filled out."

"When is the next plane landing?" Someone onboard would have a pen. I would beat her at her own game, after all.

"Hmm, I'm not sure. Maybe three or four hours. But I don't know. It is not my job to keep track of when de flights come in and out of here."

The ship would be gone by then. I would have to call my boss back at showband headquarters in Miami and explain why I missed the boat. I could say the plane was delayed. No, he would be able to call and check on the flight. I could say a taxi broke down.

But it wouldn't matter. The ship I was boarding was taking seven-day cruises. I would be stuck in Nassau at the height of the tourist season. I would have to pay for food and a hotel room for seven days until the ship was back in port. This wasn't going to be cheap.

All over a stupid effing pen. A pen that she had right there in her hand. A pen that was less than a foot away from me. A pen that, to me, was worth—oh I don't know, maybe a thousand dollars or so.

I snapped. I felt a surge of adrenaline; my heart rate went into overdrive. I'm certain that my face went red. I took a few deep breaths to keep myself calm. "This is ridiculous. I want to speak to your boss."

"You need to lower your voice. Go sit over there." She pointed toward a line of chairs in the back of the terminal. Then she tucked her pen into her little shirt pocket and waddled away.

I walked toward the line of chairs, but didn't sit down. Surely her boss would have some common sense. He would be reasonable, go fetch me a pen, and this whole wacky episode would be over.

She returned with a man in tow: linen pants, linen shirt, leather sandals, big white smile. He walked through the customs gate. "So, another one without a pen." Then he laughed and motioned toward me. "Come with me. We have a place where you can wait."

I picked up my bags and followed him to a tiny room on the side of the building. Plaque on the door said something like: *CUSTOMS HOLDING ROOM.* There was a small desk in the front of the room: deep-blue-sea-colored carpet, bright white walls, two metal chairs in front of the desk—the kind of chairs designed by chiropractors to keep them in steady supply of clients with chronic back pains.

"Have a seat," the man said and motioned toward one of the chairs. I sat down and put my bags beside me, keeping them close. He sat on the edge of the desk, one leg hanging off the ground a little. He leaned forward. "Seems like we have a little problem here."

Yes. I had a problem. I was trying to enter a country where the locals were fiercely territorial over effing pens. I looked at the desk. There was a coffee mug with an illustrated palm tree and a slogan plastered across the front in bright yellow letters: *WELCOME TO THE BAHAMAS! EVERYTHING'S MUCH BETTER IN THE BAHAMAS.* "I just need a pen."

The man leaned back, then stood up, and started

pacing around the room with his hands behind his back, as if in deep thought. As if I had just asked him some complex riddle that he was trying to solve. "Why have you come to the Bahamas?"

I felt as if I was in one of those cop movies. It had all the right components. The crime, the holding cell, now I was in the scene where they interrogated the bad guy, maybe rough him up a little. It even had the two cops. Good cop, bad cop. Except, there was no good cop. This was bad cop, bad cop.

"I'm boarding a ship."

"What kind of ship?" He said it in the way that the lead investigator on *CSI* says, *Where were you on the night of June 25, 1994?*

"A cruise ship."

"Uh-huh. And what do you do on the ship?"

"Come on. I just need a pen. There's a whole mug full of pens right there. Right in that—"

"What do you do on the ship?"

"I'm a drummer."

"What kind of drummer."

"A drummer that does the laundry. What? A drummer that plays drums. In the band."

"We're going to have to search your bags."

"Really? Geez, go ahead."

As he rummaged through my bags, taking every single thing out one at a time, he kept asking me questions. *What's my name? Where was I born? Am I sure?* I was starting to get worried. Could this all really be over a pen? Did I trigger some type of alarm in the back office? Did I look like some big-time cocaine smuggler they'd been trying to snag for years? (I *had* once been mistaken in an airport for Joey Lawrence—you know, the guy from that TV show *Blossom.* But that's another story.)

This could be serious stuff here. I might end up in the slammer over a case of mistaken identity. And not just any prison, but a Bahamian hoosegow where I'd serve a life sentence living off my one meal a day of watered-down conch chowder and grapefruit soda, and where they have a special cell in the psychiatric ward for all the other gringos who didn't have an effing pen. After about five minutes, the woman walked back in. I noticed this time that she was wearing a name tag.

"*Mrs. Gafondo,*" I said, emphasizing her name. "Would you be so kind as to pass me a pen, Mrs. Gafondo?"

She smirked.

I tried again. "Mrs. Gafondo, is it actually legal to hold an American like this over a pen, Mrs. Gafondo? Mrs. Gafondo, would you please pass me one of those pens there on the desk?"

She whispered something in the man's ear, and

they walked out of the room together. After a few seconds, the man walked back in, grabbed one of the pens from the mug, and tossed it over to me.

My belongings were scattered all over the desk. No cocaine anywhere. I was starting to think I might make it out of this place alive. I pulled the chair to the edge of the desk and filled out the form as well as I could, my hand shaking from the adrenaline come-down. "Follow me," the man said.

We walked to the customs security station. "Passport please?"

I didn't say a word. I just slid my dark blue booklet across the counter. He grabbed the stamp and punched both documents. He slid them back to me and put out one hand, motioning toward the other side of the gate, toward freedom, toward a land filled with pens and pencils and crayons, toward the cruise ship that was leaving port in an hour. I ran as fast as my little legs could run.

A half hour later, I was walking up the gangway, and I had my bags, my passport, my liberty, one hell of a story, and a little souvenir that I had tucked into my pocket before I left the Customs Holding Room—a little, stupid, plastic effing pen that read *WELCOME TO THE BAHAMAS! EVERYTHING IS MUCH BETTER IN THE BAHAMAS*.

TWO

THE CASE OF THE CRUISING, CARPING CRUMPET MUNCHER

I know this might be hard to believe, but sometimes passengers on cruise ships complain about things. Yet, no cruise ship passenger has ever mastered the art of whining like the woman that you are about to meet.

It was a sea day (a day on the cruise ship where we don't stop at any ports). We were cruising in the South China Sea, passing through the Philippines on our way to Hong Kong. I had been on the ship for nearly two months at that point, and I was bored out of my mind. So a shipmate pal and I hatched a plan. We decided to pose as passengers and sneak into teatime in the passenger dining room. We just wanted a little excitement I guess, something different to break up the monotony of living and working on a cruise ship. We also really wanted some decent quality caffeinated beverages, since the only coffee we could find in the crew area was made from a concentrated coffee syrup that was about as tasty as the water you would find blasting out of a whale's blowhole. And since we had been subsisting for the last two months off of food in the crew mess, which had all the wonderful culinary qualities of water-logged hardtack, we had both developed an obsession with getting our grubby little fingers on a few of those tasty looking cucumber-and-butter finger sandwiches served at teatime. And maybe a couple of those raisin scones that all the crew members kept smuggling from the dining room kitchen and then bragging about around the crew mess dinner table.

We sat down at a tabletop in the back of the dining room. I was sitting next to a woman wearing a bright purple, wide-brimmed hat. We had apparently joined the table at the exact moment that they had become involved in a rather violent buttered-crumpet feeding frenzy. The woman turned to me and said, "I am very unhappy with this cruise."

I wanted to ask her if she would trade places. I could take her spacious passenger cabin with room service and a balcony, and she could learn what it's like to live in a crew cabin down on deck Z, where the only thing that separates your bunk bed from the cruise ship engine is a two-inch thick wall that has the sound insulating properties of a hand-knitted Christmas sweater. But then I remembered that we were incognito, so I bit my tongue. "So what's wrong with the cruise?" I asked.

"This cruise is just too long." I had certainly heard some pretty stupid complaints from passengers in the past. One of my favorites was when a passenger complained that the ship was "just rocking too much"…in the waves…of the ocean…as we were sailing through a storm. And this passenger complaint surfaces much more on a cruise ship than you would probably think. Passengers want to sail out at sea, but they don't want the ship to rock. Oh no, that just isn't acceptable. Another one of my all-time favorite complaints goes something like this:

Passenger: Excuse me do you work here?

Me: Yes, what can I help you with?

Passenger: I have a complaint.

Me: Oh, boy! It must be my lucky day! What is your complaint, sir?

Passenger: It's too hard for me to find my cabin on this ship.

Me: Well, I'll let the shipbuilders know right away, sir. Maybe when we're in port in St. Thomas we can put the cruise ship in dry dock and reorganize the cruise ship so that your stateroom is right next to the gangway when you get back aboard the ship.

Passenger: Oh, that would be great. Thanks.

Another top-notch grumble occurred while I was walking through the passenger dining room on lobster night and overheard a passenger complaining about how he couldn't order a couple of corndogs for dinner. I guess we can't blame him. I'd rather eat corndogs than some of the lobster tails I've been served on cruise ships too.

But not once in my six-year career had I heard anyone gripe about the fact that the cruise was too long. I thought about some of the crew members aboard that cruise ship. Some of them had been cruising for nine months straight. Now that's a long cruise. That's something to complain about.

I had to know more. I turned to the woman and, with crumpet crumbs falling from my mouth, asked, "Why do you think the cruise is too long? What's wrong with a long vacation?"

"I hate going on vacations for more than five days," she replied. "I just get so bored, and I start to miss my poor dog."

I wanted to throw her overboard. I wanted to take her to the front of the ship and grab her waist and let her hold her hands out to her sides while she shouted "I'm the Queen complainer of the world!" and then just lift her up and throw her right over the bow of the

15

cruise ship. Passengers can be absolutely maddening. But don't get me wrong, we crew members love you passengers. After all, you make all of our ship lives possible. We respect you, but you can drive us absolutely banana cakes sometimes. Speaking of banana cakes, why don't cruise ships ever have banana bread for the crew? I'm going to have to write a complaint about that and send it to the head office.

THREE

MAN OVERBOARD

People fall overboard once in a while. It's just an inevitable fact of ship life. But you never expect it to happen to someone you know, especially not a fellow crew member.

I wasn't on the ship when he went overboard, but I had just left. I still had some friends in the crew of the ship where it happened, so I heard about it pretty much as soon as the guy went over the rails. I'll report to you exactly as I heard it:

It was New Year's Eve, so naturally the crew had spent most of the day and night trying to break the Guinness World Record for how many cranberry vodkas can be consumed by one single shipboard crew in twenty-four hours. By midnight, most of the crew was about as drunk as a Floridian at a Jimmy Buffet concert, or just a Floridian in general. Twenty minutes after the balloons dropped and the confetti came down and the bottles of Duck Nipple champagne (the cruise ship's official bubbly of choice) were popped open, one of the Russian dancers in the production-show cast had the bright idea that he would prove just how macho and ballsy of a Ruski he really was by doing handstands on the railing of the crew deck—at the bow of the ship, roughly five decks up, so about forty feet from the ocean.

Everything was going great. He was displaying how he was perfectly capable of balancing on the rails, holding himself in a handstand as the ship carved its way through the Caribbean Sea. Even though he had consumed nearly an entire bottle of fermented potato juice at this point. Then he showed the quickly gathering crowd how he could balance with only one arm. *Look mama! One Hand!* Amazing!

Then he slipped and fell overboard. Luckily he didn't bash his head against the side of the ship or crack his skull on a set of the ship's metal railing as he sailed down toward the cold sea below. He made a rather small splash and then started drifting fast. The crew members on deck watched in horror as he zipped past the portside hull. They quickly gathered as many life preservers as they could find on deck and threw them overboard. Someone was smart enough to send several crew members running down the breezeways on several decks of the ship, throwing out life rings as they went. All along the back wall of the crew deck, they found a line of storage containers that were stuffed with life jackets. Most of those were tossed overboard too. There are just never too many floatation devices bobbing around when you are adrift in the middle of the Caribbean Sea.

They watched as their friend, the Russian dancer—who just hours earlier had been spinning and jumping on stage, laughing and singing to a hokey rendition of "What's the Matter With Kids These Days" from the musical *Bye Bye Birdie*—was disappearing into the dark Caribbean night. He became nothing more than a small speck beneath a dark sky of twinkling stars. And then suddenly, the crew members couldn't tell what was him from what were the stars glittering out in the waves. And then he was gone.

When the captain was informed, he immediately turned the ship around, turned on the shipboard floodlights, and used the spotlight on the bridge to scan the sea for the drifting Ruski *twirlie* (ship lingo for dancers, male or female).

Talk about a party foul. Nothing in the seven seas brings a shipboard party to an end quicker than someone going overboard. That'll sober up a crew. The captain and his officers plotted a chart, analyzed the currents, determined the ship's exact location when the fellow went over the rails. While looking for the vanished dancer, the captain was just as worried about the guy drowning as he was that the ship might run him over, or worse—accidentally suck him into the propellers (it happens, folks).

Two hours after the dancer took his tumble, a rescue boat found him wearing one of the lifejackets that the crew members had thrown overboard. He was treading water and nearly exhausted. From the side of the ship, crew members used the onboard pulley system to hoist the rescue boat back on board.

Kids, don't try this on your next cruise. He was lucky, and as a dancer, he was exceptionally fit. Most people who fall overboard aren't near as fortunate. Some people end up as shark food. Many drown or die from hypothermia. The bottom line: many people who fall overboard are last seen drifting out to sea and then never heard from again.

It's a big ocean. We are small people, and—I can say from personal experience—definitely incapable of treading water as long as a twenty-three-year-old dancer who has more muscle mass in his pinky than most Americans have in their entire upper body. So what's the lesson from this story? I'd tell you not to get drunk and try to do handstands on the cruise ship railing, but I'm not an idiot. I've worked on cruise ships long enough to know that kids these days aren't going to listen to that kind of advice. So, here's the lesson: If you plan on going on a New Year's cruise, make sure your friends know where all the extra life vests and life rings are located on the open decks. Oh, and get some decent dancing lessons before you walk up that gangway. Knowing how to dance a good tango is apparently adequate shark repellent. However, I wouldn't risk falling overboard if all you know is a smooth salsa or a nice rhumba. Sharks love those kinds of dancers.

FOUR

I'LL DRINK YOU UNDER THE LADLE

On one contract, a crew member I worked with found a giant ladle in his crew cabin. It was a big wooden spoon that had been carved in Russia. A crew member must have picked it up when the ship made a stop in St. Petersburg, and then abandoned it when it was time to pack up and ship out. It could hold about a quarter-cup of rum. At the time, and since we *were* cruise ship crew members, we thought it was the perfect size for taking shots. My liver still won't talk to me due to the abuse I inflicted upon him.

FIVE

NO MOVIE FOR YOU

The rules on cruise ships can drive crew members absolutely bonkers.

It was a slow cruise. We were floating around the Caribbean somewhere. After four or five months, most of us guys in the showband had grown tired of most of the ports. When we were in Cozumel in Mexico and Ocho Rios in Jamaica, we caught up on sleep or spent some time working on our tans on the cruise ship sundeck instead of going ashore. It was simply more relaxing and interesting to watch paint dry on the crew deck than it was to get off the boat and fight the crowds of passengers. We called these *sleeper ports*.

I woke up in the middle of the day, as showband guys do, feeling as if I had drunk an entire fish tank of cranberry vodkas the night before—which I possibly

23

had, and I'm talking about one of those impressive floor-to-ceiling fish tanks that you find in fancy seafood restaurants with names like The Captain's Table and The Barnacle Pit.

The phone in my crew cabin rang. It was Marvin, the trombone player in the band. "Hey, you want to catch a movie in the theater?"

The cruise ship always has something going on: shuffleboard playoffs, bingo marathons, hairy chest competitions, Chocolate melting cake–eating contests, unclog-your-stateroom-toilet tournaments. This kind of stuff keeps going even when the ship is in port. Believe it or not, some of the passengers hardly ever get off the ship when they take a cruise. The show must go on, and so movies are shown in the main theater.

"What movie are they showing today?" I asked.

"*Shutter Island.*"

An escape. That was exactly what I needed. "I'm in."

Nothing sounded better than to sit in a dark room and watch a movie, to feel as if I was back on land, doing something that might bring a bit of normalcy back to my life.

I met up with Marvin and a few other showband guys. We walked into the dark theater. The place was pretty much empty, but we wanted to be respectful, so we took a seat in the back of the room. There was a

Filipino crew member walking around, passing out paper cups of popcorn. I grabbed a cup of popcorn, pulled a soda from my pocket that I had smuggled into the theater, and then popped the top.

When the movie started, I was transported back home for a moment. I forgot all about the shipboard politics that were driving us all crazy. I forgot all about the crummy roommate I had been partnered with in my tiny crew cabin. I just crunched on the popcorn, sipped my soda, and let *Shutter Island* steal me away for a moment. It was heaven on ship. An island of refuge from my ship life.

A few minutes later, I felt a tap on my shoulder. I looked up to see an Indian security guard. He had a dim flashlight in his hand. He shined it into my eyes, blinding me. In his Indian accent, he said, "You. All of you. You are not allowed in the theater during movie time."

"What?" Marvin asked. "We're in the showband. We aren't crew. We're staff." Staff members were the middle class of the cruise ship ranks. Officers above. Crew below. We had shipboard privileges that reflected our middle rank.

"I know," the security guard said. "You have to leave, now. Movie time is for passengers and officers only."

We got up and trudged out of the theater. We

couldn't believe it. We were in the band. This was the theater where we entertained more than a thousand passengers every single night. And now we were being kicked out. It was the rules.

That night, we were called into the staff captain's office. Each of us was given a written warning for trying to catch a flick on our time off. After a bit of halfhearted protest and attempts to explain our reasoning, we all signed our written warnings and then walked back to work, in the theater that we had just been banned from, to perform another show for thousands of passengers.

Ship life. No movie for you.

SIX

THE WELCOME ABOARD SHOW

Being the new guy on a cruise ship was a very bad thing. It meant that every morning for the first few weeks I had to pull myself from my berth, all sleepy-eyed and drowsy, and drag myself into a cramped conference room right next to the crew bar.

I was like a salmon, mindlessly, instinctively returning to my native stream. I had been home, at the only local watering hole aboard the ship, just a few hours earlier. Now all the new crew members were expected to pry their eyes open, swallow their hangovers, sit in a darkened room, and watch a film about cruise ship safety while the vessel mercilessly tried to rock us back to sleep as it rolled over the swelling waves of the Tasman Sea. I had been here before, many, many times, at the start of each contract.

I knew that these safety videos were about as exciting as a trip to a maritime museum with the world's largest collection of rusty fishing hooks. The acting was so forced I worried that the actors might be hostages.

A new girl sat next to me. She was a cute young blonde: big sky-blue eyes, thin lips, upturned nose, sexy English accent. Maybe this cruise wasn't going to be so boring, after all.

A uniformed Italian officer with a cappuccino in hand and olive oil moisturizer in his hair stepped to the front of the room. "Some of you-ah may not-ah take-ah this cruise ship safety-ah seriously-ah. Maybe the crew-ah on the Costa Concordia felt-ah the same way as you-ah. So I have brought in a little video-ah to show you-ah the reality-ah of living and working aboard-ah the cruise ship-ah." Scowling, the Italian officer took a loud sip from his cappuccino and looked across the room, like a warden looks over a room of prisoners who have just arrived at his prison to serve out their life sentences. He shook his head in disapproval. "Enjoy."

The lights were dimmed. Little, round curtains were drawn over the portholes. The officer walked over to the video player and pressed play. While the introduction credits rolled, I took my chance to talk to the new girl with the Buckingham Palace accent—not the servants' type, the posh one reserved for the people who don't know the definition of the word "job".

"Is this your first contract?" I asked. I looked down at her name tag: *ARIEL NORTHSTROM. HAIR STYLIST. ENGLAND.*

"Yes, my first day."

She smiled, but under those bright blue eyes, she looked a bit scared. I remembered what it was like on my first day aboard a cruise ship. I was quite worried too.

"Did you just graduate college?"

"Yeah, my first time away from home."

I could hear the narrator of the safety video in the background saying something like: "When you first join the crew of a cruise ship, you imagine all the fun you are going to have, all the beaches you are going to visit, all the new places that you are going to see. You never expect to *die!*"

That got our attention. I watched in shock as the narrator detailed a cruise ship accident that occurred back in the early nighties aboard the *Scandinavian Star,* a ship that was sailing out of Norway. There was a fire on board in the middle of the night. Many crew members and passengers died from smoke inhalation as they slept or while they were trying to escape.

The survivors of the fire awoke to the horrifying reality that their luxury liner was now adrift in the middle of the Skagerrat Strait. To top it all off, the captain and the ship's officers had abandoned ship before all of the surviving passengers had been evacuated. They were marooned by their own captain and navigational crew.

I looked over at Ariel. She had her hand over her mouth. It looked like tears were welling up in her eyes.

She looked at me. "Has this ever happened to you?"

"No. You'll be fine. Don't worry." My words seemed to have the same comforting effect as the bunk beds that crew members sleep on.

Welcome aboard, Ariel. Welcome to ship life. Don't forget to wear your life jacket to bed.

SEVEN

HOW TO GET LUCKY LUCKY ON YOUR CRUISE VACATION

On a cruise ship, you can get lucky, or you can get *lucky lucky*.

And the first step to getting *lucky lucky* is to make friends with the guy that operates the trash incinerator. Go down to deck zero. Turn right. Go past the crew office, and then just follow your nose. Follow the scent of rotting vegetables, day-old chocolate melting cake, and burning plastic. It'll never lead you astray. Turn right into the little room that smells about as good as the Great Pacific Garbage Patch—yes, the room with the conveyor belt filled with garbage and the massive metal bins of sorted plastics, glass, metals, food, and paper products. Somewhere in that maze of flotsam, you'll find a man diligently working his daily twelve-hour shift among the stinky rubbish. That's your best friend on the ship. Or at least he should be, if you want to get *lucky lucky*.

Introduce yourself. Laugh at his jokes. Compliment his gelled hair and rubber gloves. Bring him gifts of air fresheners for his office, the little dangling ones that smell like coconuts and pineapples and are shaped like palm trees. Take him out to dinner at the crew mess, on you. Buy him drinks in the crew bar. Sing karaoke duets alongside him to Brittany Spears' "Hit Me Baby One More Time" at crew parties. You know, wine and dine him. Be an ingratiating suck-up if you have to. Whatever it takes. Just make sure and become his *paisano*. Because the trash man isn't just the trash man. He lives a double life. He's a cruise ship double agent. Mr. Lucky Lucky.

He runs a small but remarkable store, right out of his crew cabin. And inside, you will find a constantly rotating inventory: new bottles of suntan lotion, cruise ship key chains, unopened bottles of rum, woven sun hats, a trash bin filled to the brim with sunglasses, T-shirts, bow ties, silk ties, suit jackets, pricey Cuban cigars still preserved in plastic cases, packs of cigarettes, and lighters, lighters, lighters of every size and color.

In his store, he hawks the abandoned, the left-behinds, the thrown away bits and bobs that are tossed in stateroom trashcans once the cruise comes to an end. It all goes somewhere. It all goes to the trash incinerator. It all glides down the conveyor belt and passes directly in front of Mr. Lucky Lucky on its last voyage in this world. And he has the whole trash world in his hands. Sometimes he plucks these unwanted items from their fiery fate and gives them a life anew, a life on the shelves of the Lucky Lucky store, where crew members can browse the rows of the unwanted vacation remnants.

But why do they call him Mr. Lucky Lucky? Why is it called the Lucky Lucky store? Because every time a room steward finds another pair of sunglasses in the trash; every time a bartender discovers another lighter that has been forgotten at his cruise ship saloon; every time the trash man finds another Cuban cigar drifting toward the flames and plucks it out of the heap of rotting ice cream cones with sprinkles, they have all dug out a nugget of cruise ship gold, and they all say the same thing, "Lucky, lucky! Lucky, lucky!"

EIGHT

JAMAICA ME CRAZY

So you finally made it to Jamaica, huh? Finally sailed into port in Ocho Rios, and you're about to walk down that gangway, right? What are you going to do? Margaritaville, just a few steps from the dock? Or maybe jump off the thirty-foot high waterfall at the Blue Hole? Or perhaps buy a pound or two of pot from a local who looks like a Bob Marley clone and then stuff it down your underwear and smuggle it back onto the cruise ship, right?

First two, good choices. Not great—I'd actually recommend the Italian restaurant (yes, the Italian restaurant in Jamaica) that's up on the hill from the port. Just ask around. The locals will direct you to a group of guys who are ready to mug you. Then after they take everything you own, ask them where the

Italian restaurant is. Keep a credit card stuffed in one of your socks so you can pay for the meal. There's only one good Italian restaurant in town. They'll know which one you're talking about. Nice guys.

That last idea, though—the one about a few pounds of swag bags in your panties? Hmm, that idea is about as bright as trying to fix the wiring to the cruise ship propeller before you turn off the backup power generator. *Hey, wait a minute. I swear my hand was just right there. Weird.*

Back in my cruise ship days, I always wanted to start a crew newspaper and call it *The Dickensian Times.* Tagline: *A Nautical Newspaper that's Widely Distributed as Toilet Paper.* It would report on all the happenings on the ship, everything upstairs and downstairs, from the lido deck to the bilge tank, port to starboard. All the articles would be reported from a crew member perspective, of course. I'm sure it would win all kinds of literary awards.

However, it would be a bit repetitive. This *is* ship life that we would be reporting on. If anything, ship life is tiresomely monotonous. But this would come with some rather enjoyable benefits. For example, we would be able to run the same story every time we are in port in Jamaica, which would read something like this:

OCHO RIOS, JAMAICA—A couple of moron *cones*

(that's passengers, in cruise ship lingo) were apprehended at the gangway this afternoon after a strip search revealed that the two American teenagers from Nebraska were attempting to smuggle two pounds of marijuana aboard the *MS Barnacle*. Once again the German Shepherd K-9 unit alerted the local Jamaican police, who were operating the search and seizure unit, of the approaching marijuana forest while the two passengers were still a half-mile from the ship. The police agent's second clue to the possible poorly-thought-out drug smuggling operation was that both teenagers, one male and one female, looked stoned out of their minds. The third clue came when the officers looked down at the teenage smuggler's pants and saw a rather unnatural pouch, similar to that in which kangaroos carry their young. When one of the officers pointed to the kangaroo stomach of one of the passengers and asked what it was, the passenger replied, "Hey, man. Like, relax, dude."

The police officer's suspicions were further increased when the Jamaican police officer suddenly recognized the cruise ship passengers from Nebraska as the two *gringos* that he had sold four pounds of marijuana to only a few hours earlier.

Mr. Puji Bayani, the Indian security guard at the scene of the arrest, reported to us that the marijuana was unmistakable. Bayani said, "It was wrapped in Bob

Marley T-shirts and tied around the passenger's waists. There was even a trail of pot behind them where some of it had fallen out as they walked up the gangway. But I wouldn't take my word for it. I have been hallucinating because I haven't slept in three days as a result of my work schedule. Thank you."

The Nebraskans were handcuffed and taken to a Jamaican jail, where they were tortured with a never-ending loop of the Bob Marley song "Stir It Up" played through loudspeakers. Eventually the two tourists caved, and had their parents wire two thousand dollars each to the police officer's bank account, at which point they were released and managed to jump aboard the *MS Barnacle* seconds before it sailed from port. They spent the rest of their cruise in the brig, where they were served lobster and chocolate melting cakes and other food that was leftover from the passenger dining room menu each night.

Now you, the reader, might be feeling like this is all just the stuff of fantasy on my part. Au contraire, mon frère. Passengers were not arrested for trying to smuggle pot aboard the ship *every* time I was in port in the Rastafarian country, but it did happen quite often. You would think that passengers would realize that maybe, just maybe, the captain would think to increase security at the gangway when we are in port in a country widely known for a religion that literally centers around getting stoned. But no, the *cones* (passengers, remember?) keep stuffing it down their pants.

And while many passengers may not be so bold and brash as to attempt to smuggle the marijuana back onto the ship, many of them definitely want to spend a few bucks and maybe buy a joint or two from a pot peddler on the street. It makes sense. When in Rome, right?

Wrong.

I'll let you in on a little secret. Don't buy pot from anyone near the port. I never did this, but I heard the stories from passengers and crew members who did, and most of them ended up forking over a lot more than the going rate for whatever it was they wanted to buy. These Jamaicans have a racket, a sting operation of sorts, and this is how it works:

1) You're walking down the street of Ocho Rios, minding your own business, when a guy with dreadlocks down to his feet, a lazy twinkle in his eye, and a big trustworthy grin asks you if you want to buy "some ganja, mon".

2) You look around and think, *Why not?* You give the guy a few bucks, take your jazz cigarette and attempt to go on your way, headed toward some secluded oceanfront hillside where you can puff

the magic dragon.

3) You walk two steps, and a local Jamaican guy who bought a cop uniform at a Halloween shop jumps out of the bushes, and throws you against the wall. The next thing you know, you're being handcuffed and thrown into the backseat of a rusted out Chevy Malibu that's spray-painted white and black like one of the cop cars from the 1980s cop show *CHiPs*. You think the car must be authentic, because it has one of those mail-order blue cop lights plugged into the cigarette lighter—the same rotating blue light that the Jamaican cop uses when he doubles as a DJ after the sun goes down.

4) You marvel at the length of the cop's dreadlocks. You think, *Wow! Even the cops have dreadlocks in Jamaica.* Then Mr. *CHiPs* starts to interrogate you as he drives around in circles in a scummy neighborhood approximately twenty-five feet from where you were arrested. He informs you that you're going to spend the rest of your life in a Jamaican prison living off a diet of Red Stripe that does nothing but dehydrate you and Jamaican jerk chicken that's way too spicy for anyone to actually swallow. You'll live this way for several miserable years until one day you give up and die. The official diagnoses on your death

certificate: *Insanity induced from overexposure to "No Woman No Cry."*

5) But he gives you a way out. If you pay him six hundred fifty dollars and buy him a beer at Margaritaville, he'll let you walk free.

6) You cough up the ransom and are thrown out of the spray-painted cop car at the foot of the gangway.

7) You never go to Jamaica again for as long as you live, and just to play it safe you decide to take cruises that only sail to Eastern Caribbean ports—which, in my honest opinion, is what everyone should be doing to begin with. Remember: eastern, not western.

The bottom line: there's absolutely no reason for this to take place at all. I'll let you in on another secret here. If you're that dead set on smoking grass, grab a taxi and tell the driver to take you to Bob Marley. That's right. In Jamaica, Bob Marley isn't just a man, he isn't just a legend—he's a destination. Leave early for the trip, though, because it's a bit of a hike from Ocho Rios, taking about an hour each way.

The cabbie will take you to a place called Nine Mile, up in the mountains, in the St. Anne's Parish. Once there, you'll find a little bright yellow schoolhouse, as well as the birthplace and final resting place of the legendary Reggae musician, Mr. Bob

Marley. Once you walk inside the gated walls of the community, you'll discover an entire herd of people willing to sell you more smoke than BP used to smoke up mirrors during the BP oil spill (FU, BP). And no fake cops. Just do yourself a favor, leave the bud in Bob Marley, and you'll make it back on the ship in time for the early dinner seating in the passenger dining room, and without the stopover and bribe routine in the Jamaican jailhouse. My suggestion though: skip all that junk and go to the Italian restaurant on the hill, and then take a cab to the Blue Hole, jump off the waterfall, swim in the grotto behind the falls, tip the local kids well, and leave the weed for the dreadlocked locals. Or better yet, take a cruise that doesn't go to Jamaica at all.

But if you're already on the ship and you're headed that way, just stay on the ship and watch a movie in the main theater. Even sitting through *Santa Claus versus the Martians* for the third time is better than most port days in Jamaica.

NINE

THE WORD ON THE SHIP

One day, as I was changing out a painting in the art gallery, this passenger approached me. He must have been about eighty years old, and he was wearing a tweed jacket with leather elbow patches. Rather stylish chap. He walked up and whispered in my ear, "The word of the day is *legs*." He backed away and then looked right at me, keeping a straight face the whole time.

Naturally, I was creeped out. I thought he had either lost his marbles or was some sort of senile version of James Bond. Then, a slow smile crept across his happy, wrinkled face. He pointed to Gertie, my girlfriend at the time who worked with me in the art gallery, and said, "Spread the word."

TEN

I GOT THE SHOWBAND BLUES

Musicians can get bored with music. It happens. They fall into a funk that they just can't shake, and then they start to consider a serious career change into something slightly more financially stable, like selling nutritional supplements and protein powders with one of those pyramid scheme companies that one of your friends is incessantly talking about very excitedly for a month or two until they realize that there is absolutely no money in it. And nowhere in the world is this Acute Musician Boredom Disorder (clinically known as AMBD) more frequently diagnosed than on cruise ships.

I think someone made a commercial for a medication used to treat AMBD once. The long frightening spiel at the end of the television ad where the drug companies are required by law to disclose any dangerous side effects went something like this: *Musicians in cruise ship showbands are statistically at higher risk of developing AMBD. Common side effects include nausea at the sight of your sheet music, violent vomiting when exposed to any music associated with shipboard production shows, tremors during passenger talent shows, immediate-onset migraines and Tourette's-type outbursts whenever you are asked to play "The Greatest Love of All" for the millionth time, as well as headaches and blackouts and phantom body pains whenever performing hip-hop segments or Broadway show-tune sections of onboard production shows. Be careful when taking medications for AMBD. Don't take medications for AMBD if you are currently taking medications to treat depression or chronic frustration as a result of performing jazz sets or Dixieland band concerts on the promenade, as these may cause complications with AMBD medications that could lead to severe and prolonged illness, including heart attacks, stroke, cancer, death, and throwing your shipboard music director overboard.*

I know about AMBD firsthand. I once tried to work aboard the same ship for eight months straight. After a few months, I started memorizing where all the tiny coffee stains were located on my production show sheet music. After three or four months, I began assigning specific notes and rhythms to said coffee stains. After I reached the six-month mark, I started playing little competitive games against myself while I was performing. First, I simply challenged myself to play the show as perfectly as I could. Then I started adding little difficult drum fills here and there, just to make the show more challenging (which is something that lead trumpet players just adore). However, most of the time I was just on autopilot. I would put on my headphones and wait to hear the prerecorded signal that signified that the show was about to start: "One, Two, Ready, Play." Then I would drift into some sort of utopian daydream which often involved several or more cruise ship showgirls, those feathery outfits with thongs and wings and thigh-high boots they sometimes wear, and a tub of cocoa butter. And then suddenly I would come back to reality just as I was hitting the last note of the show. Autopilot can be a very enjoyable experience if you know how to fly your plane right.

It was on this eight-month-long contract that the music director for the showband must have started to see the early signs of AMBD in several of the showband guys. One day he showed up to rehearsals carrying a miniature-sized basketball goal (the kind with a suction cup on the back of the hoop) and a small, orange foam ball. While the orchestral pit (a hydraulic stage that can be dropped into a hole that is called the pit) was lowered, he walked to the front and center of the pit and stuck the basketball hoop right to the front wall, right in front of the guitar player.

He walked over to his chair in the front left corner and made a perfect throw, nothing but net. "One."

Then he turned to the band and smiled. "I'm as bored as you guys. Now we have something to do during the shows. Everybody keeps their own score. The ball gets passed down the line. Whoever scores the most points gets free drinks in the crew bar after the show, on me."

We all laughed.

The he added, "We just have to remember two things. Take the net down before the stage goes up at the end of the show so that the goal doesn't get crushed. And don't throw the ball so hard and high that the audience can see it or that it ends up in the crowd."

It was quite fun to see the inventive ways that musicians devised that enabled them to throw a foam ball with one hand while still hitting the right notes, chords, or rhythms in the production shows with the other hand. The bass player, keyboard player, and I probably had it the easiest. I could play some of the drumming in the shows with one stick and still manage to score a goal every blue moon or so.

Truth be told, I was pretty crap at pitball, but some of the guys in the band really made some amazing plays, stuff that should have been recorded and re-aired on the SportsCenter Top Ten. Production shows had never been so much fun.

And no medication necessary. Just a little ingenuity, a couple of kids' toys, and a brilliant leader who was willing to break all the rules. Our brave music director was fired three days later.

ELEVEN

IS THAT OUR SHIP...
SAILING AWAY WITHOUT US?

Sometimes you miss the boat. Yep. You went to the local Margaritaville to blow off a little steam because you really thought you were about to go insane. You drank a stream of Hurricanes more potent and dangerous than *Katrina* and *Ivan* combined until your mouth turned red. And then you started watching clocks on the walls—the ones always on five o'clock— to decide when you should start stumbling your way back to the cruise ship gangway.

At half past six, the bartender finally cut you off and informed you that the sound you have been laughing about for the past half hour, the one you thought sounded like the biggest fart you ever heard in your life, was actually the ship's horn blowing the final all-aboard. You run as fast as your little legs can run, all the way to the end of the pier, and watch as your cruise ship drifts away from the dock, all your friends and family smiling and waving, pointing and laughing at you from the lido deck.

Passengers miss the boat. Crew members do too. The difference here is that passengers have paid for the cruise. When *they* miss the ship, it's their responsibility to find their way back. They can catch a flight and catch up with the ship in the next port. Then just walk up the gangway and buy another piña colada, have a laugh about their misadventure, and then dance the rhumba up on the lido deck and move on with their lives.

Not so for crew members. Crew members are paid to be on the ship. They are under contract. And they are told that under no circumstances are they to miss the ship—captain's orders. So when it comes to finding their way back on board, crew members are in pretty much the same position as passengers and have to pay their way back home, which is not a nice prospect for a Filipino room steward making four or five hundred dollars a month.

These desperate times sometimes call for desperate measures. And that is where our hero comes into our story. We will call him Jack—that sounds dashing and bold and hero-like, doesn't it? Well, I knew Jack. I worked with him on a cruise ship that was sailing around Alaska one summer. He wasn't a guy to exaggerate or tell tall seadog tales about his days sailing on the blue highway. No, he was a pretty trustworthy fellow, and he had one story that he loved to tell.

We'd buy him a few Stella Artois in the crew bar and take him out to the crew deck where we could gaze out over the choppy sea and feel the wind on our faces, and then a shipmate would often say, "Jack, tell the story again about the time you missed the boat." Someone would of course say, "This is a ship, not a boat." And then Jack would stare off toward the distant horizon and tell his one, signature, sea story which went something like this:

"I was taking a taxi back from Red Hook, the water taxi port on the eastern shore of St. Thomas that leaves from Red Hook Bay. My girl and I had spent the day on St. John: snorkeling, hiking from beach to beach, drinking beer, getting tan. On the way back to the ship, our taxi broke down. We were way up on the hill. The driver said he was going to have to get his taxi towed. He wouldn't even refund our money. We had been in the taxi for quite a while—had made it past Anna's Retreat, already turned onto Weymouth Highway. I figured we were no more than three miles from the harbor south of Charlotte Amalie. After deciding to leave the broken-down taxi behind, we set out on our own, walking back toward the port.

"It was about two o'clock in the afternoon. Our back-on-board time for crew was two thirty. The ship was sailing at three. We pretty much gave up hope for making it back on board by the crew all-aboard deadline. We knew we were going to lose our ship IDs. Security would take them away as soon as we walked up the gangway. I felt like that was a huge price to pay for being late, but I knew those were the rules, and so I was prepared to spend the next two weeks or so trapped on the ship. But I didn't want to miss the boat.

"We tried to flag other taxis down as we walked along the steep road back to port. It was torture, really. Whenever we made it over a hill, we had this awesome view of the Caribbean from our elevation. We could see the cruise ships down in the harbor. I felt like I could reach out and touch them, but they were still so far down the mountainside. All the safari taxis (the open-air taxis that you find in the Virgin Islands) were packed full of school kids in their uniforms who were heading home from school at this time of day and tourists heading back to the ship. We walked for about forty-five minutes until we were finally picked up by a safari that let us cram in with a bunch of locals. The taxi dropped us off in front of the port. We could hear the ship blowing its horn. The security guards were laughing and moving slow, talking in their island style so that we couldn't understand what they were saying. I think they were trying to hold us up. They wanted to look through everything we had.

"They finally let us go, and we raced toward the pier, past the girl handing out free coconut smoothie samples, past the souvenir shop, past the steel drum band at the second gate at the foot of the pier. Once we reached security there, I could see that we were too late. The ship was drifting away from the dock.

"I couldn't believe we had missed the boat. What were we going to do? We didn't have our passports. The crew office had them. They had taken them, just as they take every crew member's passport. I had made the stupid mistake of leaving my only other form of ID, my driver's license, on board the ship. We wouldn't be able to fly anywhere. We were grounded. We had a couple of nearly maxed-out credit cards and about forty U.S. dollars between us. I was going to have to call my parents and try to have them wire me some money somehow. We were going to have to spend the next seven days in a hotel while we waited for the ship to sail back into port. This was going to be very expensive. A nightmare. Then again I could think of worse places to spend a week off from work. At least we weren't trapped on Rabaul or in Jamaica.

"I desperately looked around the port. I don't know what I was looking for: some sort of way out I guess. More like a way back on board that ship that was slowly, very slowly, sailing away. Could we swim out to the ship? No, that would be too dangerous. And we'd never be able to catch it.

"Then something caught my eye, but it was on the other side of the harbor. I explained my plan to Jennifer"—his girlfriend at the time—"and we ran off to the other side of the wharf, where we found a local fisherman. He had an onboard radio on his small fishing boat. I asked him if he could contact the cruise ship. I explained our situation and my plan, and he said he'd help us for thirty bucks. We agreed and forked over our crumpled wad of U.S. bills. We even included a ten-dollar tip. He radioed the cruise ship, explaining that he had two crew members that had missed the boat.

"We hopped in his little fishing vessel, and he bounced over the waves at top speed until we were right next to the cruise ship. I watched as the gangway opened. I could see two Italian officers waiting inside the ship. They were waving their hands telling us to come on board. I don't know what I expected, but it wasn't this. The fisherman steered his boat right beside the cruise ship, small waves rocking the tiny craft back and forth. He got as close as he could, and the officers yelled over the ship engines, telling us to jump. We walked to the lip of the fishing boat and jumped one at a time. I went first. I was nervous as hell, but I was more frightened by the amount of money I was going to have to spend if I didn't make this jump.

"I bet we set world records for the standing long jump that day. I jumped as hard as I could and landed just at the edge of the gangway. The officers grabbed me and pulled me inside, laughing their asses off. Same for Jennifer. She almost slipped when she hit the edge of the gangway, but one of the officers grabbed her before she fell overboard.

"The staff captain wasn't laughing when he called us into his office. Our ship IDs were taken. We didn't touch land for a whole month. It was hell, being on that ship for that long without some shore leave. But you know what? I'd do it again in a heartbeat. I never felt more alive than when I was jumping across that open water and jumping back aboard that ship. I never felt so cool. It was some real James Bond–type stuff. I'm fairly certain it was illegal, too. But I don't think the officers ever told anyone else what they had done. Ship life. Crazy."

So don't miss the boat, folks. Unless you got a local fisherman with a sturdy vessel and a crazy look in his eyes and a real good long jump up your sleeve. In that case, do it. But know that you might not live to tell the tale, like Jack did. And more likely, they won't open the gangway for you, and you'll be out forty bucks or so.

"Ship life. Crazy." No other three words have ever been spoken that were oh so true.

TWELVE

SHOOTIN' STINGERS

Next time you go see a show on a cruise ship, make sure and look down in the orchestral pit before the show starts. The band will be warming up, but look closely. Most of the guys in the showband will be looking around in the audience. They're looking for beautiful women. How do I know? Because I used to be down there with them.

On one contract, one of the guys in the band read the book *Ball Four* by Jim Bouton. In the book, Jim says that baseball players used to do something called "shooting stingers". They would look around the stadium and look for a good-looking gal. If they made eye contact with one, they would stick out their tongue. If the girl looked away, it meant she probably wasn't interested. If she smiled, or even better, stuck her tongue out too, it meant the ballplayer might have a chance. I never tried it. I thought it was dumb. Some of the single guys in the band were always trying it with pretty passengers in the audience. They said there was something to it, although I'm not sure what kind of girl you're going to attract by sticking out your tongue. I don't have any real firsthand experience. I dated a dancer most of the time I worked on the ship.

So, just for fun, let's do a little experiment. If you're a pretty female and you're reading this book, next time you go on a cruise ship, you should stick your tongue out at the showband drummer. Then send me an email and let me know what his reaction was.

THIRTEEN

CLARENCE KNOWS
HIS TV PEOPLE

It was a case of mistaken identity, and it had happened before.

I was transferred—again. But I didn't want to go this time. I was happy where I was, working on a ship plodding around the Caribbean, going to the east and then west, back and forth. A lovely way to spend a winter. A lovely place to avoid shoveling snow. I had been called up to a different ship that needed a drummer quick. It was supposed to be a nicer ship, one that was out of Tampa, a ship with a supposedly better route. But I didn't want to go anywhere. I had just fallen for a gorgeous brunette, a Canadian dancer: the sort of Canadian beauty that made me willing to travel to the ends of the earth to get her that *poutine* she was always talking about, the kind of Canadian sweetheart that made me want to give up my U.S. citizenship and trade my beloved Starbucks for a lifetime of Tim Horton's. She was that pretty, that type of goodhearted cruise ship showgirl.

When it was time for me to leave the ship, I considered hiding in one of the lifeboats. I'd be a stowaway. I'd live off of stale ice cream cones and dusty bottles of Duck Nipple champagne that my Canadian cutie smuggled into my hideout every night. I didn't care. I just didn't want to leave that girl.

But then the day finally came, and I started thinking about the reality of the situation: she'd end up dating an Italian officer if I lived in a lifeboat. The officers had much nicer rooms, and I'd probably start to smell like a passenger aboard Noah's ark after a few weeks.

So I reluctantly said good-bye. Kissed her one last time, and I never saw her again. Typical ship romance. Typical young fool who always thinks he'll meet another girl somehow. I should have rolled the dice and camped out in the lifeboat. I'd have a beard to my knees, a life-threatening case of scurvy, and a severe alcohol dependency from years of champagne guzzling, but I probably would have been a lot happier than where the cruise ships ended up taking me.

When I arrived at the airport, I dragged myself up

to the security station. There was a friendly guy working there. It was about four in the afternoon and my flight wasn't until nine. I had plenty of time to kill, so I waited until the security line was empty to go through. I put my bags up on the conveyor belt.

The man looked at me and then started pointing. "Hey, I know you. Aren't you on TV or something?"

I laughed. I wished. I would've been making a lot more than the peanuts that the cruise ship companies were paying me to wear a monkey suit and play drums. "No. I've never been on TV. You got me confused with someone else."

He kept pointing. He gave me that look that people give you when they are letting you know that the two of you are sharing a secret. "No. I know you. You're a TV star. On one of those big TV shows."

He turned toward the lady who was working at the X-ray machine. There was no one else in line, so it wasn't as if there was some sort of rush to get me through the security station. "Hey Charlene! Come over here for a second."

Charlene was a big girl. I patiently waited as she waddled our way.

The man turned to her and said, "Look at this guy. Don't you recognize him? Isn't he on some TV show?"

Charlene looked me up and down. "These TV people. Always saying they're not who they are.

Always trying to pull a fast one on us. Yeah, he looks like someone I've seen before. He's a TV guy, for sure."

"But which one?" the man said.

"I don't know. But I've seen him before. On TV."

The man put out his hand. "I don't believe you," he said with a smile. "You mind if we take a look at your license?"

I pulled out my license. I was sure once they read my name on my official ID, *JOSHUA LAWRENCE KINSER*, this whole discussion would be over.

The man took a look at my ID, and his eyes lit up with excitement. "I knew it! I knew it!"

"Who is he?" Charlene asked, leaning over to see my ID card.

"Joey Lawrence."

"What?" I asked.

He repeated it. "Joey Lawrence. That guy from that TV show about that nerdy girl. What was it called? *Flower*?"

"*Blossom*?" I asked.

"Yeah, *Blossom*. That's it. Joey Lawrence from *Blossom*. You think you're smooth. But you can't trick ol' Clarence. I know my TV people."

Charlene raised her eyebrows and nodded. "Yep. That's right. Clarence. He knows his TV people. They always try to sneak through here. But Clarence, he catches 'em. Every time."

Clarence pulled out a piece of paper and a pen. "How about an autograph?"

"You got me," I said, and I grabbed the pen. I signed it: *To Clarence, You sure know your TV people. Joey Lawrence, the guy from Blossom. Whoa!*

FOURTEEN

I'M TIRED
AND I WANT TO GO HOME

Crew members love to go home. In fact, once aboard a cruise ship, there's nothing a crew member loves to do more than leave. We count the months, then the days, then the hours, the minutes, the seconds.

And then finally we are walking down that gangway, running for the tarmac, dashing for that plane that will lift us off that hot runway that's out in the middle of some Caribbean island and fly us through the clouds until we are back home. Leaving the ship becomes an obsession for each and every crew member that has ever worked below the waterline.

I was at the end of my contract, a long dreadful contract in which I had made a good bit of money but would have traded it all for a decent home-cooked meal and a room that didn't make me feel like I was living inside of a Cold War–era submarine.

The ship was scheduled to go into dry dock, so most of the crew was leaving at the same time. We were all huddled in a passenger dining room, bright and early in the morning, most of us still hopelessly drunk and without a wink of sleep as a result of the celebrations that always ensue when a crew member knows they'll be saying good-bye to ship life for a while once the sun comes up.

We were a rough-looking lot: dancers still wearing their show makeup from the night before, which had smeared badly from all the crying they were doing as a result of having to say good-bye to the other girls in the cast, casino dealers still in tuxedos and bow ties who smelled like the wet bar in a rock star's dressing room, and then a few of us showband guys who looked rather perky because we usually didn't go to sleep until around this time in the morning. After all, the only way for a showband guy to eat breakfast in the crew mess is to stay up until five in the morning. Nobody wants to live without bacon for eight months.

We were gathered together in the passenger dining room, waiting for the immigration officers to show up. It's a cruise ship tradition to gather all the disembarking crew members as early as humanly possible in some random dining room somewhere and then make them wait for six or seven hours until the immigration officers show up. It's the ship company's way of saying, "Thanks for all the hard work. You did a great job. Now hurry up and wait one last time, because we find it hilarious to make you do this."

I wouldn't be surprised if the CEO of some of these cruise lines has a video feed from these dining rooms that he can watch on big sign-off days for the crew. He probably gets a kick out of watching everyone go insane after waiting for the immigration officers for hours on end.

Of course, the crew doesn't mind. We're used to this kind of nonsense. At this point, we don't care about anything. Our bags are packed. We've said our good-byes. All we have to do now is walk down that gangway and...freedom! Glorious, liberating, sunbeam shining down on us from heaven, *freedom!*

I was talking to a group of dancers—all from England or Australia, all finishing up a very long nine-month contract—when the staff captain walked up to us. He was holding a radio, and he did not look happy. "Excuse me, but there seems to be a bit of a problem."

Had someone died back home? Was the ship sinking? No. It couldn't be. I was supposed to be eating a roast dinner and sleeping in my very own bed in a few hours.

"What happened?" a dancer asked.

"Well, a volcano erupted and—"

"What?" was pretty much the general response.

The staff captain put out his hand to calm every one down. "Now hold on. No one has been hurt. This is in Iceland. A volcano in Iceland has erupted and—"

Everyone looked relieved. "So what does this have to do with us?" I asked.

"Just let me explain. A volcano in Iceland has erupted, and the ash plume is enormous. All flights from here to England have been cancelled."

I was sure that one of the dancers was going to faint. Instead, she gathered herself and asked, "For how long?"

"They don't know."

"What do you mean, they don't know? Can't they just fly around it?"

"No. The volcanic eruption is that large. And they have no idea how long it's going to last."

"Any idea. Days? Weeks? Months?"

"Unfortunately not. However, there is some good news."

"Okay," the dancer said.

"Since the ship is in dry dock, everyone who has a cancelled flight will be able to stay aboard the ship until they are able to fly home." This was about as good of news as being told that your entire family fell overboard somewhere off the coast of Antarctica. Dry dock: going on a cruise inside of a jackhammer on a ship that sails to nowhere and all the passengers are replaced with construction workers whose greatest intellectual achievement is perfecting the whistle they use to try and get the attention of every woman that walks by. The only time a destination of dry dock is good news is when you are just released from a high-max prison, and then it's pretty much same old, same old.

The dancer's jaw dropped "This is a joke. This has to be a joke. Are you pulling my leg? Ha! You almost had me there."

The staff captain looked down at the deck. "No. This is not a joke. We'll let you know as soon as we hear anything else. But for now, I would suggest that anyone scheduled to fly to England today return to their crew quarters. You are not flying home today."

Those dancers had been counting down for nine months. Now they had no idea when they were going home.

Those dancers ended up having to spend an entire week aboard the dry-docked ship. It nearly drove them mad. After a week in dry dock, they would have rather been thrown into the erupting volcano than spend another day aboard that ship.

The Icelandic volcano finally sputtered out and stopped disrupting international flight patterns for a bit. There was probably an entire plane full of English cruise ship crew members headed back to England that day. As they were flying over Iceland and spotted the still smoldering volcano, they probably all said some very choice words that cannot be repeated here— words to express their extreme gratitude to the volcano gods, of course.

FIFTEEN

SO, FERDINAND MAGELLAN AND CAPTAIN CRUNCH WALK INTO THE CREW MESS...

On one contract, we had some pictures hanging in the crew mess. They were mostly nautical scenes, ships battling the ocean and that sort of thing. On one wall there were a few portraits of famous sea captains: Lord Nelson, Francis Drake, and Ferdinand Magellan. A group of the guys in the band and I were in the middle of very long contracts. We were all starting to turn into sea donkeys, which is what happens when you stay out on the ship too long and start to get a little crazy, a great deal stubborn, and so bored that you resort to all sorts of random mischief.

The guitar player hatched a plan. We used the

printer in the crew office and printed out portraits of Captain Crunch and that sailor on the front of the box of Gorton's Fish Sticks, the guy with the yellow rain slicker and rubber wellingtons. We tacked them on the wall right next to the Ferdinand Magellan portrait. For three days, every time we went into the crew mess, we would see that line of portraits: Lord Nelson, Francis Drake, Ferdinand Magellan, Captain Crunch, the Gorton Fish Sticks guy, Popeye. We couldn't spend more than five minutes at a time between laughing so hard we cried our tear ducts dry. No disrespect was meant to any of the admirable sailors. In fact, we hadn't completely transformed into full-fledged sea donkeys yet. We still had some healthy boundaries intact. The proof is that we were going to include a portrait of Edward John Smith, captain of the *Titanic,* but we thought that this might be crossing some sort of watery line. I think we were right.

SIXTEEN

YOU GET TO CRUISE FOR FREE BUT HERE'S THE CATCH

A cruise ship is one big maze. If you look hard enough, you can find quiet spots on the ship that are difficult for most passengers to find, little nooks that are off the beaten path. When I first climbed aboard a ship that was scheduled to sail north from New York City into Canada, I immediately set off to explore the crew area. I was searching for the perfect place to read, a quiet breezeway or open deck where passengers couldn't find me and ask me stupid questions. I finally discovered this one tiny deck on the back of the ship that was really difficult to get to. You had to take several different staircases up and down decks and then cut through a passenger area just to reach it. It looked like the perfect spot to read. You could look out over the wake of the ship and see the sky above. It seemed really off the radar for most of the crew.

But there was a problem. Every time I went out to that deck at night, I would find the same group of four or five Filipinos sitting out there smoking. They had pulled a few deck chairs from the lido deck and kept them close to the ship's rail. I returned every night, hoping to find a time when no other crew members were out there, but those same Filipinos were always there. After a few visits, I started to notice something odd. Every time I walked through the door that read CREW ONLY and out onto the open area, one of the Filipino crew members would pick up a broom and start sweeping the deck.

This happened every time I went out there. I knew something was up, so I kept visiting the back deck every night, always looking for something out of place.

One night I found it. I noticed that a rope was tied to the ship's rail. I walked over and looked down. The rope stopped about halfway to the water, and attached to the rope was some heavy-duty fishing line.

I asked the Filipinos if they were fishing. They said they were catching all kinds of stuff and having the crew chef cook it up for them. The lengths crew members will go just to get a decent meal in the crew mess.

SEVENTEEN

LET'S TACO BOUT
THAT CANCUN COFFEE

You should always know the exchange rate in the country that you are visiting when you're on a cruise. Yes, I know you are on vacation and you're enjoying that temporary lapse in judgment where you allow ten-dollar piña coladas to be charged to your "emergency" credit card—the one with the forty-five percent interest rate.

You don't have to act as if you're Donald Trump just because the air temperature is twenty degrees warmer than where you live, but most of us walk up that gangway and leave everything we ever learned about managing our finances (most of it from reading *Dilbert*) back at the cruise ship terminal at the Port of Miami. We let our guard down, and we put that voice in our head that we call common sense on mute. We don't want to just get away from our busy lives for a few days. We want to escape completely.

When I'm on a cruise as a passenger, I do the same thing. I mean, it's not as if the cruise ship company has some kind of ploy to create an environment where they have a captive audience that they can pillage and plunder like a band of ruthless pirates any and every chance they get. No, cruise line executives are responsible, caring, generous people who simply want you to have the best vacation that you can possibly have while drinking margaritas from exhaust funnel–shaped glasses with about as much alcohol content as the pool water on the lido deck and which cost about as much as an appointment to get your teeth cleaned.

While you're on the cruise ship, you should just relax and sip, sip, tip, tip away. (Specifically remember to tip the showband drummer.) It's when you stray from the protective bosom of the cruise ship hull and the defensive shields of the cruise line's Italian officers that you should put your wallet in your front pocket, learn to say "no" very firmly in whatever language the locals speak, and always, always know the exchange rate. Especially when you're traveling to the one place where overcharging is as common as aggressive men asking you if you want a taxi or a cigar or both, where boundaries are loosely defined by exactly how much tequila has been consumed in the past twenty-four hours.

Of course, I'm talking about none other than our friends to the south: Mexico.

Now, don't get me wrong. I'm not trying to pick on Meh-hee-co. I love the fact that you can make every single one of their cultural entrées out of the same five ingredients just as much as the next guy. But after five years of cruising to ports in the land of enchantment, I've learned a few things, *mi hombre*. There is an American coffee shop in Cancun that is very popular with cruise ship passengers. These passengers travel for two days out at sea. They travel to a land full of unique and rare cultural treasures and sights to be seen. They could go and see the Mayan temples of Chichén Itzá, or the drunk Americans at Carlos and Charly's, but first they all want to get a decent cup of coffee, something impossible to find on a cruise ship unless you prefer coffee that tastes like a delightful combo of teak oil and brass polish. The lines at this coffee shop sometimes wrap around the building and are a testament to the power of caffeine and just how boring Cancun really is. I would do it too. I wanted a good cup of coffee, and I wanted the free Internet, so I'd wait in that line.

We were in Cancun every four days or so, and after a month of going to that coffee shop, I stumbled upon a genuine act of chicanery. I had just checked the exchange rate online before I walked into the coffee shop. I was actually interested in buying a large shipment of Mayan hammocks while I was down in Mexico and was hoping to smuggle them back into the states and then make what I thought at the time would be a fortune, selling them at farmers' markets and craft fairs across the US. I wanted to be quick with the exchange rate when I negotiated with the local hammock boss.

The coffee I ordered was priced at fifty-two pesos. The young woman behind the cash register said "Five dollars." I handed it to her and took my coffee. As I walked back to my table, I calculated the exchange rate. My coffee should have cost only four dollars.

As I sat at that table, I watched every customer come through the line, one after the other. I listened to what they ordered and calculated the rate of exchange. The baristas were rounding every sale up—usually by an entire dollar, sometimes more. I watched fifty people go through the line in just an hour. This shop must have served at least five hundred people per day, which meant that practice brought the shop five hundred *extra* dollars a day. I got back in line, and when I got back to the register, I told the woman that I had been overcharged by a dollar. I also told her I didn't think it was right for her to overcharge every customer.

She pulled me aside, and after trying to dissuade me with some math that was as fuzzy as a peach skin, she said, "What do you want?" I told her I wanted free coffee. She handed me a stack of at least thirty cards, each one good for a free coffee. Who says you'll never use math in the real world?

I continued to calculate the exchange rate every time I found my ship roped up in Mexico, and I was always very well caffeinated when I did.

EIGHTEEN

THE TIP OF THE DRUMSTICK

The first book in my *Chronicles of a Cruise Ship Crew Member* series seems to have started something. In the book, I encouraged passengers to start tipping crew members a little better. My intention was to help increase the tips that the waiters, room stewards, and bartenders received, especially the crew members from places like the Philippines and India. However, since the book was about my experience as a drummer in the showband, I started receiving emails from readers who were inspired to tip the drummer in the band.

Now I've started a collection of photos that passengers send me of showband drummers holding twenty-dollar bills. If you're on a cruise right now, tip the drummer, your room steward, waiter, or someone who has made your cruise extra special, and get a picture of it. If you send it to me, I'll tack it on the wall in my writing room. The pictures make me laugh out loud, and they remind me that we can make a difference, however small, in someone's life—one cruise ship drummer and one cruise ship crew member at a time.

NINETEEN

YES, YOUR CRUISE SHIP SHORE EXCURSION WILL INCLUDE NEAR-DEATH EXPERIENCES

A friend and I were on a cruise ship that was sailing around Australia. We were leafing through a glossy booklet of shore excursions that the ship offered. It was all the usual stuff: snorkeling the Great Barrier Reef, riding dune buggies through a dusty desert in the outback, zip-lining in the Blue Mountains, visiting the aborigines who really know how to play a mean didgeridoo in Sydney Harbor. Nothing was really jumping out at us.

But then I stopped flipping through the pages, brought them to a sudden halt. I was looking at the excursion of a lifetime. It was titled *Adventure to Death*

Swamp, and then below that, *See the Horrifying Jumping Monster Crocodiles.*

The pamphlet was littered with crisp color photos of crocodiles seemingly in midflight, their tails completely out of the water as they soared upward and latched onto a bloody hunk of cow tongue that some smiling Aussie, with a crazed look in his eye, was dangling over the side of a pontoon boat. Onlookers cheered and gawked at the carnage and at the incredible feat of reptilian acrobatics. It all looked exceptionally dangerous, extraordinarily violent, and remarkably pointless.

We signed up immediately.

The field trip was supposed to take us deep into the outback of Aussie-land, to some murky river that runs through an eerie swamp, the kind of place that kangaroos go when they've decided to give up on life. Once there, we would board a rickety pontoon boat and allow two complete strangers to guide us into the darkly depths of crocodile country in search of some of the most violent creatures on planet Earth.

It all sounded too good to be true. When the day finally came, I packed a bag of peanuts in case I got hungry.

Waiting for us outside of the ship was a remarkably new and safe-looking bus to take us into Australian no-man's-land. Our driver was a friendly and animated man with leathery skin that was the same shade and texture as his leather hat, which even had a hatband of crocodile teeth. He reminded me of Crocodile Dundee—not the original one, but the version of Dundee that might have been cast in a low-budget sequel that went straight to on-demand video. He kept us mildly entertained with stories about his not-so-wild adventures in the Australian outback which always seemed to end with him having a campfire and spending the rest of the night drinking Foster's beers the size of oil cans.

When we reached the swamp, the driver veered from the paved road and took us onto a dusty gravel lane that cut straight through the heart of the swamp, a vast expanse of shrubby tropical plants and inky, still water that stretched to the horizon on both sides of the country road. I found myself daydreaming as I looked out the bus window and over the boggy Australian landscape. I imagined what type of frightening creatures must lurk below the surface of the creepy marsh: swamp snakes, bloodsucking spiders, cold-blooded crocodiles with a discerning taste for American flesh made sweet by a steady diet of chocolate-covered donuts and dollar-menu cheeseburgers, wild-eyed kangaroos that could box like Muhammad Ali (float like a bush fly; sting like a wallaby)—kangaroos that had been driven to insanity long ago by the recurring concussions caused by weak-armed boomerang enthusiasts.

That's when the bus ran right off the road, drove straight through the barbed wire fence, and toward the edge of said swamp. I heard screams. The driver yelled, "Crikey!" and lost control.

The bus careened into the same swamp that had been so benignly described in the pamphlet as none other than "Death Swamp".

The bus nearly flipped over onto its side. I heard the sound of safety glass shattering into tiny dull-edged squares, more screams, and then the most cursing in more different languages than I've heard since I went on the Log Flume ride at Disney World. Someone in the back of the bus immediately kicked out the back window. The driver told us to get out of the bus and to go stand on the dirt lane. My friend and I climbed through the back window and trudged through the swamp toward the road, fully expecting to be devoured at any moment by a massive Venus flytrap or confronted by a crocodile who at that very moment had decided to end his month-long fast and give the new Atkins diet craze a whirl.

We made it to the road, and I checked to see if all my limbs were still attached to my body.

A few minutes later, a truck arrived to shuttle us to the rickety pontoon boat so we could watch the crocodile version of Hungry Hippos. The crocodiles did "fly" out of the water, using their powerful tails to thrust them from the river. My friend and I shared my bag of peanuts as we watched the crocodiles' teeth chomp onto the cow tongues that were dangled over the side of the boat by the same crazy-looking Aussies we had seen in the glossy pamphlet.

All in all, it was the best excursion I ever went on. However, next time, we decided we'd just play it safe and go visit the Sydney Opera House or something.

"Crikey!"

The following is an excerpt from:

CHRONICLES OF A CRUISE SHIP CREW MEMBER

ANSWERS TO ALL THE QUESTIONS EVERY PASSENGER WANTS TO ASK

A nonfiction book by Joshua Kinser

Now available at Amazon.com as an eBook and in print

INTRODUCTION

I never expected to find myself out at sea, unless that Mississippi River rafting trip I always wanted to take went way wrong. Somehow, I ended up working on cruise ships for more than five years. It was the wildest time I have ever had. For someone who is absolutely addicted and entirely obsessed with traveling, there is no better job than working on a cruise ship. As a travel writer working for magazines and guidebooks, and as a musician in touring bands and on cruise ships, I have been able to travel all over the world. I can honestly say without a doubt that a cruise ship is one of the most fascinating places you can visit. However, a cruise ship is more than just a ship. It is a city. As crew members, we are living aboard these floating cities that charge through the sea and rope up at port after port, beach after beach, and paradise after paradise. And just like cities, cruise ships have their own unique language, culture, personalities, their own bright side and even their own dark side as well. It is immensely interesting.

When crew members go out to sea and choose to work on a cruise ship, they aren't only working on the ship. Crew members are living on that cruise ship, spending most of their time in the crew areas beneath the water line that often are as fascinating as they are crowded. In this book, I would like to take you on a tour of a crew member's life and show you what it's *really* like behind the scenes aboard one these massive, metal, party ships.

A cruise ship definitely is an interesting place to live, and people (landlubbers especially) seem to harbor a curious fascination with the sea and those who venture into its waters—a fascination that will live on forever. There is a reason that people today are still mesmerized by the *Titanic*. And if you choose to go and work on a cruise ship, taking a job out at sea will naturally stir up the curiosity of those around you. From the time you set foot on a cruise ship, your life will never be the same again. For starters, it will be a life filled with questions about what it is like to work on a cruise ship. Your friends, family, and even complete strangers will want to know what you experienced out at sea. Even on my first day as a cruise ship crew member, passengers wanted to know the inside scoop. Everyone wants to know what happens down in the crew areas.

I wrote this book to answer all of these questions once and for all. However, allow me to give you fair warning before our story at sea begins. While it is easy to romanticize about what it must be like to live on a cruise ship from the comfort of your favorite armchair, believe me, working on a cruise ship is definitely not all frozen daiquiris and midnight buffets. I wrote this book about what it is *really* like to live and work aboard a cruise ship. So, this book does steer away from idealizing the ship. This book tells the complete story. And this means that the book is going to describe both the positive and the negative sides of ship life. Some people may be surprised to learn that many crew members have a deep love-hate relationship with the cruise ship, but it's true. I will explore this complex experience. I will explore all of the luxurious and incredible parts of working on a cruise ship, but I will also reveal the obnoxious, nearly intolerable, and downright grimy aspects of ship life as well. Some of you may not want to read about the negative aspects of cruise ships. So, this may not be the book for you if you want to read a book that takes place in a fantasy land where all of the Filipino cabin stewards on a cruise ship are happy, smiling crew members who burp butterflies, fart rainbows, and make towel animals solely because they love to see passengers smile. And you should probably move on if you are a cruise ship employee or a veteran cruiser who would be upset by a story that makes a cruise director look like a complete boob. However, if you want to hear both sides of the story, the positive *and* the negative, then keep reading.

I am sure that some crew members may disagree with what I have written. They may disagree with my perspective of the ship. But I am equally sure that most crew members will be able to read this book, nod their heads, and say, "This is exactly what it is like." However, I can only draw from my own experiences, and so I can only tell this story from my perspective. Yet, no two crew members are going to have the same experience. In fact, no two cruise ships are alike. This is because every ship has a different captain. Every crew member has a different attitude. Each cruise line has different rules for their employees, a differing approach to ship design, and a different style of management. There are also different crew members on every ship. A crew member can return to a cruise ship they worked on just a year earlier to find that the ship is nothing like the one they remember. And most importantly, there are hundreds of different jobs on a cruise ship, and a crew member's job will largely define what kind of experience they have. I worked on cruise ships as a musician in the lounge bands, jazz trios, and orchestras. My experience was undoubtedly very different than that of an officer working on the bridge, a cabin steward in housekeeping, or an engineer in the engine room. Yet, we all experience ship life together—the same wonderful experiences as well as those miserable aspects too.

No matter how you feel about what I have said in this book, I sincerely do hope that you find the book entertaining and one that you enjoy. I see my experience on the cruise ship through a comedic lens, and so I hope you are able to read the book with this in mind. This is a book that I am certain will leave you with a deep sense of what it is really like to work on a cruise ship. It will show you that working on a cruise ship is a lot like sailing in rough seas; there are a lot of ups and downs. And after you read this book, I guarantee that you will never be able to hear the deep and thundering sound of a cruise ship's horn the same way again. Now, let's untie this vessel from the safety of the dock and see what adventures lie ahead.

Joshua Kinser
September 7, 2012

1

WHAT TIME IS THE MIDNIGHT BUFFET?

About two weeks is the breaking point. At least that's when I hit my breaking point on my first contract. Let me explain. There are 200 or more cruise liners that are floating out at sea right now. On each of these cruise ships there are 2,000 passengers, on average. This means that at any given moment, there are more than 400,000 passengers wandering around lido decks, standing in the hot sun waiting for a lifeboat drill to start, or searching for the next buffet. And there is one thing every crew member learns very quickly on a cruise ship; every passenger has potential—potential to ask a crew member a stupid question. And most passengers absolutely live up to this potential. Sometimes, it is the repetition of the questions more than the fact that they are painfully idiotic that drive crew members over the edge. These questions can often be enough to send crew members heading straight for a gallant leap over the rails of the ship and into the dark blue waters below. In those cold waters, crew members will at least find bliss in the certainty that there will be no passengers, and certainly no one asking stupid questions.

Questions like, "What time is the midnight buffet?"

"Is there an elevator that goes to the front of the ship?"

"Where's my cabin?"

"What do you do with the ice sculptures once they've melted?"

"Why can't I drink alcohol at the emergency boat drill?"

"Do I have to go to the mandatory boat drill?"

"Does this ship generate its own power?"

"Do the crew members sleep on board?"

When crew members are asked their first idiotic question, they usually stop in mid-stride as they are walking down the promenade and wonder whether they have made the right decision to go work on the seven seas. Crew members will question whether *they* are in fact the idiot. The idea to get a job on a cruise ship sure sounded great when they first visited the cruise ship recruiter's office. The recruiter made it sound like crew members do nothing but get paid to sail around the world and visit sunny beaches across the globe. The recruiter made working on a cruise ship sound more fun than an eternal ride on Space Mountain at Disneyworld.

I hit my breaking point about two weeks into my first contract. I'm pushing a cart, one similar to the luggage carts you find in a hotel lobby, and it's loaded down with a poorly balanced assortment of drums and other music equipment that could topple at any minute. I'm a drummer in the orchestra, or showband as it is often called, and so I'm one of the musicians you see if you watch any of the production shows in the main theater. If you're on a cruise right now, we're the ones dressed in all black like we're going to a funeral, the ones walking around like we don't have anything to do. If you don't see any of us, go and check in the crew bar. We are probably in there drinking.

The showband is also the backup band for the

various entertainers that perform aboard the cruise ship. This includes singers, magicians, jugglers, contortionists, banjo players, and accordion virtuosos (yes, there is such a thing, and it can be painful to watch). The showband also performs jazz sets in the cigar bar and a variety of other styles of music in the different venues around the ship. The orchestra is kind of the work horse of musicians on the ship— the one-stop shop for all your musical needs.

I was trying to move my drum set to the atrium for one of our biweekly jazz sets. We actually played more of an odd mix of funky tunes and Dixieland classics, but we'll call it jazz for the sake of simplicity. For these jazz set gigs, I had to move my entire drum set from one side of the ship to another twice a week.

Have you ever tried to walk from one end of a cruise ship to the other as fast as you can? If you're on a cruise right now, go do it and come back to me. Ok, that wasn't much fun was it? Remember all those people walking around aimlessly that were in your way? You know how I know all those people were there? Because they are always there. The *cones* are always there. On cruise ships, there is an entirely esoteric lingo that crew members use, and *cones* are what we call passengers. I'm not sure where the meaning derived, but I assume it is because crew members always feel like passengers are in the way, just aimlessly walking, gawking, and searching for the midnight buffet or something.

Back on the promenade, I'm pushing the cart of drums, and not a single *cone* is getting out of the way. The entire drum set had been unable to fit on the cart, so I'm also carrying a case of cymbals in one hand while trying to direct the cart through a crowd of passengers with the other hand. It was a comical course of immovable human obstacles. I make it about halfway across the ship after nearly clipping a few brightly-colored frozen drinks from a couple wearing matching tropical shirts. The couple looks like they could have come directly from a *Magnum PI* episode— one of the early ones before there was a decent budget. I continue to slowly steer my cart through the crowd, and then I see her from across the promenade. She has that look, that annoying inquisitive twinkle in her eyes. I cringe. I've been spotted and identified as an employee. I just know it. Before I can avoid her by quickly steering the teetering luggage cart behind one of the doors that lead into a "Crew Only" area, she's already across the promenade and tapping me on the shoulder.

"Do you work here?" she asks. I look at my name badge and then at the ridiculously heavy cart of drums.

"Yes Ma'am, what can I help you with?"

"Are you a musician?" I thought the name badge that clearly said "Musician" and the cart of drums would have given it away.

"Well, I guess I am," I said. The lame attempt at humor was met without reaction.

"Do you know where my room is?"

"Well, what is your room number?"

"I don't know."

Sigh… "I really wish I could help you. I have a performance in about thirty minutes, but I recommend you go to the Purser's desk. It is forward of the atrium, on the starboard side."

"Where is that?"

"Forward. Starboard. Mid ship."

"Which way is the front of the ship? Is that what you mean by forward? Star what? Where's the middle of the ship?"

This went on for five more minutes and then continued for five more years. It happened almost every time I would peek out of the crew area and find myself face-to-face with passengers. It can be exhausting, but this is part of the job. And believe me, there are many reasons to absolutely love this job. The midnight buffet is just one of them. I don't care how much people make fun of the midnight buffet. The midnight buffet is at midnight, 12 a.m. sharp, it rocks, and it is one of the great parts of working on a cruise ship. In fact, the musicians in the orchestra usually get off work around midnight, and the midnight buffet is often the first stop. Actually, there was a predictable order of events every day during the five years I worked on a cruise ship as a musician. I would sleep, eat, go to the gym, get off the ship and explore if we were in port, play music, hit the midnight buffet, party in the crew bar. Repeat for five years. However, the fascinating story of what it is like to work on a cruise ship is what happens between the obvious, and that is what we are going to explore in this book.

"What time is the midnight buffet?" was a question that never bothered me. In fact, I'm not certain I was ever asked that one. But I did reach the breaking point from the constant questions after two weeks. As a result, I, and a few other musicians on the cruise ship, joked about doing something about it. We thought it would be a great idea for the cruise company to print up some shirts for the crew to wear. We wanted the shirts to be printed with all of the stupid questions the crew gets asked, and then have extremely sarcastic answers printed below them. When we would get asked a stupid question, we could just point to the shirt and move on with our day. At one point, the company started threatening to do something entirely similar, but with the exact opposite outcome we had wanted. Some no-brain executive thought it would be a great idea to make shirts for the crew that had a giant question mark printed on them and in big letters,

"How Can I Help You?" printed on the back. The company printed some of these shirts and handed them out to a few willing crew members to test the waters. They insisted that at least one crewmember from every department would have to take on the new roll of the walking and talking customer service agent. No one in the band would volunteer. Musicians don't volunteer for anything on the ship. We have enough work keeping sharp on our instruments as it is.

Eventually, they forced one of the guys in the band to take the shirt. I think he was our bass player. He didn't go into guest areas for the next month until the program was scrapped. The shirt was then promptly thrown overboard in an elaborate, highly illegal, and exceptionally intoxicated ceremony somewhere off the coast of Jamaica. I always hope to visit Jamaica someday and see some kid wearing the shirt after finding it washed up on the shore of Montego Bay. Do you have any idea how many times that kid would be asked if he knows where to get some pot?

"What time is the midnight buffet?" is really a silly question though, because the cruise ship is one giant, floating midnight buffet. The midnight buffet is whenever you want it to be. The midnight buffet is really no different than the buffet that happens the rest of the day. Sure, there are a few lull hours when the buffet is closed in an attempt to encourage the passengers to get out and do something other than eat. But if you want to eat during the lull when the buffet is closed, there are plenty of other choices. You have the dining rooms that serve you three meals a day. Then there are the buffets that also happen three times a day in case you miss your dining room opportunities or just feel like eating six times a day while you're on vacation. If you still want to eat more, you can visit the grill on the lido deck and stuff yourself full of hamburgers, hot dogs, fries, and gyros. You have the sandwich shops and the 24-hour pizzeria. On most ships there are sushi stands, steak houses, Italian restaurants, and a window café that serves a rotating list of Asian menus.

It's insane how much food there is on a cruise ship. It really is an incredible feat. On average, 105,000 meals are prepared every single week aboard a cruise ship. This requires around 20,000 pounds of beef, 12,000 pounds of chicken, and 28,000 eggs. So before you go out on your next cruise ship and find the showband drummer just to ask him, "What time is the midnight buffet?," I'm going to save the drummer from having to answer one more question. The midnight buffet is whenever you want it to be. And it never ends.

~~~~~*****~~~~~

ALSO BY JOSHUA KINSER:

Chronicles of a Cruise Ship Crew Member: Answers to All the Questions Every Passenger Wants to Ask

The Cruise Ship Capers and the Missing Klimt: An Art Heist on the High Seas (Fiction)

Good Dog, Bad Mountain: A Memoir about a Dog, a Young Man, and a Hike on the Appalachian Trail

Monkey Selfie: A Fun Short Story about a Monkey, His Selfie, and the Legal Battlestorm that Followed (Fiction)

Hiking South Carolina: A Guide to the State's Greatest Hikes, published by Falcon Guides

Florida Gulf Coast, 3rd and 4th editions, published by Moon Handbooks

Five Star Trails: Raleigh and Durham: Your Guide to the Area's Most Beautiful Hikes, published by Menasha Ridge Press

Five Star Trails: Charlotte: Your Guide to the Area's Most Beautiful Hikes, published by Menasha Ridge Press

For a complete and up-to-date list of Joshua's books, visit his Amazon.com author page at:
www.amazon.com/Joshua-Lawrence-Kinser/e/B007Q5531I

Now that you've finished my book, will you please consider writing a review?

www.amazon.com/dp/B00PUWRW72

Reviews are the best way for readers to discover great new books. I would truly appreciate it. And thank you for purchasing and reading my book.

ABOUT THE AUTHOR

Joshua Kinser is the author of ten books, including *Chronicles of a Cruise Ship Crew Member*, a laugh-out-loud memoir about what it's really like to work on a cruise ship, which has been a #1 bestseller in Amazon's "Cruise" and "Caribbean" categories. For his cruise ship series books, he draws from his experiences working as a musician and as an art auctioneer aboard cruise ships for more than six years. He is the author of six internationally distributed travel guides including *Florida Gulf Coast* published by Moon Handbooks and *Hiking South Carolina* published by Falcon Guides. He has worked as a staff writer for Gannett with the *Pensacola News Journal* and has published articles in magazines such as *SAIL*, *Dance Spirit*, and *Times of the Islands*. He has written over 200 articles online for websites such as Trails.com and USA Today Travel.

Feel free to contact him at: **Joshuakinser@gmail.com.**

35876897R00063

Printed in Great Britain
by Amazon